Blackpool Trams & Recollections 1972

Barry McLoughlin

Contents

© Barry McLoughlin 2016

ISBN 978 1 85794 490 7

Silver Link Publishing Ltd
The Trundle
Ringstead Road
Great Addington
Kettering
Northants NN14 4BW

Tel/Fax: 01536 330588

email: sales@nostalgiacollection.com
Website: www.nostalgiacollection.com

Acknowledgements

Many sources were used in the production of this book, but particularly valuable were Steve Palmer's series of erudite volumes on the Blackpool tramway; *Blackpool Tramways 1933-66* by Stephen Lockwood (Middleton Press); *The Blackpool Tramway* (The Tramway Museum Society); the ever-informative and sometimes trenchant *Trams Magazine;* and the websites of the Blackpool Heritage Trust: *www.blackpoolheritage.com/htrust/* and British Trams Online: *www.britishtramsonline.co.uk.*

But the most heartfelt thanks must go to the late Ray Ruffell, who had the foresight to take these wonderfully evocative pictures at a time when the future of the tramway was by no means secure.

All the images in this book are from the Ray Ruffell collection, which is held by the publisher. Ray was a railwayman, transport enthusiast and photographer of equal merit who travelled all over the country in pursuit of his hobby and his art.

Dedication

To Julie Humphrey

First published in 2016

British Library Cataloguing in Publication Data
A catalogue record for this book is available from the British Library.

Printed and bound in the Czech Republic

Introduction

The year 1972 was a watershed for the tramway in Blackpool as it sought to cut costs and increase income. After a decade of decline, the local council introduced the first five of 13 new one-man operated (OMO) trams, rebuilt from old railcoaches. Their bodies were modernised and extended with new tapered cabs with front entrances; the existing doors became a centre exit.

It was the first major investment since the arrival of the elegant but ill-fated Coronation cars almost 20 years earlier, and the introduction of the high-capacity Progress twin-car sets from 1958.

After a period of stagnation, the OMO cars helped revitalise the tramway, which was suffering a drop in passenger numbers as a result of changing holiday patterns.

The experiment was not a big hit with the travelling public, however, as the trams offered a less-than-comfortable ride. But their swift conversion and introduction at a time when the very existence of the tramway was under threat provided a low-cost, albeit relatively short-term, solution to some of the network's problems.

One of the most significant of these was the decline of the traditional seaside holiday as increasing numbers of Britons chose instead to hop on to jets for package holidays to warmer climes. This in turn led to fewer staying visitors and therefore fewer customers for the trams.

Almost exactly 40 years later, at Easter 2012, the network would enter a new era with the launch of Blackpool's £100 million light rail system, complete with 16 low-floor 'Flexity 2' trams, new infrastructure and a high-tech depot at Starr Gate.

But 1972 was also a year of tragedy for Blackpool, for Britain and beyond. Three children were murdered by a doctor at the resort's Victoria Hospital, nearly 500 people died in the worst year of the Northern Ireland Troubles, and the country was ravaged by high unemployment and industrial unrest, with Prime Minister Edward Heath declaring two States of Emergency. In August, 11 Israeli athletes and coaches were massacred at the Olympic Games in Munich.

On 17 February, in one of the most sensational and horrific crimes in Blackpool's history, Dr Ahmad Alami murdered three sleeping children at Victoria Hospital, and also stabbed two nurses and other children who were asleep on the ward. Alami, the son of the Grand Mufti of Jerusalem, was diagnosed as a paranoid schizophrenic and judged unfit to stand trial. He was detained at Broadmoor for several years before being deported back to the Middle East.

On a lighter note, Blackpool Zoo opened on 6 July on the site of what had been Stanley Park Aerodrome, which was used for RAF parachute training during the Second World War and later became the home of the Royal Lancashire Show. Defying an unseasonably damp day, Johnny Morris of TV's *Animal Magic* opened the zoo – riding on an elephant and accompanied by the mayor in a Rolls-Royce.

South Promenade to North Pier

Title page: **SOUTH PROMENADE** Cabin-bound OMO car 2 and Coronation 655, heading for Starr Gate, pass near the Queens Hydro Hotel – 'Bed and breakfast £3.50' – on South Promenade on 26 August.

WATERLOO ROAD is the location as 1953-built Coronation car 661 glides by en route to the terminus at Starr Gate on 26 October. Behind the front cab is the Dutton Arms pub. The illuminated windmill at Waterloo Road, just out of shot on the left, was one of the landmarks of this section of the prom.

Photo	DESTINATIONS
1	**QUEENS HOTEL** (Title page)
2	**WATERLOO ROAD** (Previous page)
3	**WATERLOO ROAD**
4	**SOUTH PROMENADE**
5	**MANCHESTER SQUARE**
6	**SOUTH PROMENADE**
7	**TOWER**
8	**TOWER**
9	**NORTH PIER**
10	**NORTH PIER**
11	**NORTH PIER**
12	**NORTH PIER**
13	**NORTH PIER**
14	**NORTH PIER**
15	**NORTH PIER**
16	**NORTH PIER**
17	**NORTH PIER**
18	**NORTH PIER**
19	**NORTH PIER**
20	**METROPOLE**
21	**METROPOLE**
22	**METROPOLE**

WATERLOO ROAD Brush railcoach 625 waits behind 48-seat OMO car No 2, converted earlier in the year from English Electric single-decker 620, near Waterloo Road on 26 October.

SOUTH PROMENADE Single 'twin-car' 679 splashes through a promenade downpour on 27 October. This was one of the double-ended twin-cars that could operate both with trailers, at busy periods, and separately.

MANCHESTER SQUARE At Manchester Square, English Electric single-decker 614 and Brush railcoach 633 head respectively to and from Rigby Road depot on 14 May. The Manchester Hotel is on the right. Apart from the section behind the Metropole Hotel and the now-disconnected line in Princess Street to Blundell Street, this was the only stretch of street-running track left in Blackpool, but this will change with the construction of a proposed £22 million extension from Talbot Square to North Station.

TOWER Transport in triplicate: Mini estate car, horse-drawn landau and electric-powered tram… Brush railcoach 622 passes the Tower (behind the camera) on a rainswept 27 October.

SOUTH PROMENADE
With no hard hats or high-vis vests in sight, the finishing touches are put to track repairs on South Promenade before the start of the 1972 summer season. Railcoach 636 has just negotiated the works near Manchester Square en route to Fleetwood on 25 May. On the left is the converted double-decker permanent way bus. The boats seen between the bus and tram were used to take holidaymakers on pleasure trips.

TOWER A week before the end of the 1972 Illuminations, Brush railcoach 634 heads south from the Tower on 24 October. The tiger on the waiting shelter points the way to the No 21 bus to the newly opened Blackpool Zoo. Car 634 was the first tram sold for private preservation when much of the traditional fleet was dispersed to museums and private collections in the run-up to the 2012 upgrade. In 2009 it was saved and restored by Andy Ashton, who donated it to the Blackpool Heritage Trust in 2016. The trust was formed in 2014 to promote the retention, preservation and continued operation of Blackpool's collection of historic tramcars. The non-profit trust is developing an interactive visitor centre to showcase the collection and provide a permanent home for Blackpool's heritage trams. Website: *www. blackpoolheritage.com/htrust/*

Meanwhile, Fleetwood Heritage Leisure Trust, which owns several Blackpool trams, also plans to open a tramway museum as a major new attraction for the port, possibly at Wyre Dock.

NORTH PIER In this sequence of pictures, Coronation 660, now beautifully preserved as part of the Heritage Fleet, though currently not operational, is turned at Talbot Square on 18 May. In the first picture, the conductor adjusts the doors as the tram arrives.

Right: **NORTH PIER** Then, using one of the long poles that were kept at turnaround points, he skilfully manoeuvres the trolley through 180 degrees so that it is facing in the right direction. If the wheel on the trolley was not properly aligned, the spring-loaded pole could leap skywards. Pantographs don't have this problem…

Left: **NORTH PIER** Coronation 660 is ready to depart on the middle road of the three-track layout at Talbot Square. Inside, the reversible seats have also been turned in the right direction, though the destination blind will need changing.

Left: **NORTH PIER** Advertising cigarettes and the Guys and Dolls Boutique in Clifton Arcade, burned down in the Yates's Wine Lodge fire in 2009, railcoach 615 leaves from North Pier on 26 May. In 1975 it was rebuilt as one-man car No 11.

Right: **NORTH PIER** With the War Memorial and Metropole in the background – the only hotel on the seaward side of the Blackpool tram tracks – railcoach 637 stands by the shelter at Talbot Square on 25 May.

Below: **NORTH PIER** New OMO car No 2, in its striking yellow and crimson livery (or plum and custard, depending on your viewpoint) leaves Talbot Square for Bispham on 26 October. The renowned Roberts' Oyster Rooms, established in 1876, are to the left and, behind the tram, is the distinctive green honeycombed façade of Lewis's department store. The car parked almost outside the Oyster Bar is a Hillman Avenger.

Above: **NORTH PIER** The photographer's wife and daughter admire 613, one of the English Electric-built streamlined single-deckers, as it passes Talbot Square on 18 May. The tram later became OMO car No 9. The Midland Bank is now the Counting House pub, while Yates's Wine Lodge on the extreme right is an empty site after the famous bar was burned down in 2009, though plans have been proposed for a £3 million redevelopment.

Above: **NORTH PIER** Frank Carson and George Roper are among the stars appearing in the North Pier version of the hit TV show *The Comedians*. A large crowd waits by Brush railcoach 622 on 25 May, although they are not queueing for the tram but for tickets for the show, which opened the following day.

Left: **NORTH PIER** With the Tower in the background, towing car 680 pulls away from North Pier heading for Fleetwood. This was another of the twin-car trams that could operate separately without a permanently coupled trailer, although from 1972 it worked only as a 'solo' vehicle. The tram, built by English Electric in 1935 and converted in 1961, returned to Blackpool in 2015 on loan from Heaton Park Tramway in Manchester as part of the Heritage Fleet at Blackpool Transport Services.

NORTH PIER Pleasure flights around the Tower from Blackpool Airport were still a big draw in the early 1970s, before air travel became universal. They are advertised on English Electric railcoach 614 at North Pier on 27 October. Sadly, after the big airlines pulled out, the relatively new airport terminal building was demolished in 2016, though the control tower remains open for shorter flights.

NORTH PIER Work takes place on the overhead lines behind Balloon 700 as it leaves North Pier bound for Bispham on 27 October. This tram, entering service in 1934, was painted in striking, all-over green 'wartime' livery in the early 2000s, but has now been converted for operational duties as part of the 'B' fleet of modified Balloon cars with adapted doors and disabled-friendly access. It is painted in Blackpool Transport's purple and white livery.

1972
No 1 Records (1)

January
Benny Hill   *Ernie (The Fastest Milkman in the West)*
New Seekers   *I'd Like to Teach the World to Sing*

February
T Rex   *Telegram Sam*
Chicory Tip   *Son of My Father*

March
Nilsson   *Without You*

April
Pipes and Drums and Military Band
  of the Royal Scots Dragoon
  Guards   *Amazing Grace*

May
T Rex   *Metal Guru*

June
Don McLean   *Vincent*
Slade   *Take Me Bak 'Ome*

July
Donny Osmond   *Puppy Love*

August
Alice Cooper   *School's Out*
Rod Stewart   *You Wear It Well*

September
Slade   *Mama, Weer All Crazee Now*
David Cassidy   *How Can I Be Sure?*

METROPOLE Painted in all-over cream, unique Brush car 638 heads south past Butlin's Metropole Hotel, closely followed by Pleasure Beach-bound double-deck English Electric Streamliner 700, on 22 October. Car 638 had been the first to be converted to one-man operation in 1969, but the trial was unsuccessful and the tram was later scrapped. By the time this picture was taken, the front entrance behind the cab had been removed – and closer inspection reveals it's a woman at the helm.

Left: **METROPOLE** The street-running section around the Metropole Hotel in Princess Parade was a big headache both for trams and road traffic, particularly for visitors unfamiliar with the layout. On 22 October, a black cab squeezes past southbound Balloon 718 and northbound English Electric single-deck car 618. The rear destination blind seems a little confused about where the latter is heading… Fleetwood is the better bet!

Right: **METROPOLE** Today the stretch of track around the Metropole has been segregated from the road but in 1972 it was shared with cars, vans, lorries and buses. Railcoach 621 passes the Medical Supplies and Leather Goods shop on the corner of Queens Square on 22 May. Above the shop is the fondly remembered Town and Country Restaurant, on the side of which a finger-sign points to Blackpool North Station. The Princess Cinema just behind the tram is showing the film adaptation of *Steptoe and Son.*

Photo	DESTINATIONS
23	METROPOLE
24	METROPOLE
25	METROPOLE
26	METROPOLE
27	METROPOLE
28	METROPOLE
29	COCKER SQUARE
30	COCKER SQUARE
31	NORTH PROMENADE
32	GYNN SQUARE
33	GYNN SQUARE
34	GYNN SQUARE

1972
No 1 Records (2)

October
Lieutenant Pigeon   *Mouldy Old Dough*

November
Gilbert O'Sullivan   *Clair*
Chuck Berry   *My Ding-A-Ling*

December
Little Jimmy Osmond *Long-Haired Lover from Liverpool*

METROPOLE Dating from 1935, English Electric car 618 was rebuilt in 1968 with tapered front ends and longer saloons with increased capacity. However, the experiment was not a success and it was converted to become the last of the OMO cars, No 13, in 1976, but was the first to be scrapped nine years later. On 14 May 1972, it shares the road with a Ford Anglia, registration plate HTF 429F. an MGB Roadster and a Mark 3 Ford Cortina.

METROPOLE As the end of the 1972 Illuminations season approaches on 27 October, single-deck Brush car 625 passes the Metropole Hotel on its way to the Starr Gate terminus. The Princess Cinema is showing *The Godfather*, starring Marlon Brando and Al Pacino.

Above: **METROPOLE** Double-deckers at the double outside Butlin's Hotel on 22 October… Balloon 708 (left) heads north to Bispham while sister 703 makes its way south to Starr Gate.

Opposite: **METROPOLE** The sign on the left sends a clear message as English Electric car 613 enters the street-running section between Cocker Square and Talbot Square on 20 May.

Above: **METROPOLE** If hapless motorists missed the white line on the left, they could easily end up the tracks. OMO No 2 rumbles on to the street-running tracks heading for Manchester Square and the depot on 26 October.

Opposite: **METROPOLE** Against the background of the Regent Court high-rise flats near Cocker Square, Coronation 662 drifts south on 19 May. Arguably the most elegant trams ever to work in Blackpool, the 25 cars introduced in Coronation year, 1953, were 8ft wide and seated 56 passengers, and were operated by modern 'Vambac' controls. Sadly, however, the handsome trams were too heavy, electricity-hungry and possibly over-engineered for the Blackpool infrastructure, and suffered frequent breakdowns as a result of their complex control system. The first was withdrawn as early as 1968 after just 15 years' service. Cars 660, 663 and pioneer 304 survive at Rigby Road.

Left: **COCKER SQUARE** On what could be a trial or driver-training run, OMO car No 3, only rebuilt that year from railcoach 610, descends the incline near Cocker Square on 26 October 1972. Cocker Square was the northern terminus of the original 1885 conduit tramway – the world's first electric street tramway.

Right: **COCKER SQUARE** Car 618 again, this time at Cocker Square with the photographer's wife and daughter, Joan and Margaret, waiting patiently beneath the 'Polo' tram stop sign. This was a compulsory rather than request stop.

NORTH PROMENADE Packed towing car 678, minus trailer, heads south on 26 October on North Promenade. The elegant, colonnaded three-tier promenade was the location for many events, including car rallies and the Milk Race cycling tour of Britain.

Right: **GYNN SQUARE** Burdened by its roof advertising, English Electric single-decker 614 climbs from Gynn Square, North Shore, on 20 May, with the Savoy Hotel in the background.

Below: **GYNN SQUARE** Coronation 662, which can be seen in the background in the previous picture, follows 614 up the incline from Gynn Square on the same day.

GYNN SQUARE Ray Ruffell's wife, Joan, and daughter, Margaret, again wait for the tram, this time railcoach 629, at Gynn Square on 22 May, after it has just passed the Savoy Hotel en route to Starr Gate.

Bispham to Fleetwood

BISPHAM On the segregated sleeper track south of Bispham Station, 1935-built railcoach 612 picks up speed as it travels to Starr Gate on 24 May.

BISPHAM Bispham Station remains a fine neo-classical building, with its Greek columns and pediment, the northern terminus for Illuminations specials. Here it is at 5.10pm on 24 May 1972. Plans were put forward in the early 2000s for it to be restored as a centre to serve the local community. Today the station retains its three-track layout, though one of the two crossovers was removed as part of the 2008 track rationalisation.

BISPHAM With the season about to get into full swing, English Electric railcoach 613 stands at Bispham Station on 24 May with a service for Starr Gate. In the background is the former Williams and Glyn's Bank, now RBS.

Left: **BISPHAM**
The driver leans out of the cab window of Brush car 636, built in 1937, at Bispham on a blustery 24 May. The amusement arcade in the background on the corner of Red Bank Road is still there, as are the flats above, built in the late 1930s and once used by showbiz stars doing seasons at the Blackpool theatres. The arch behind the tram marks the start of the Illuminations.

Right: **MADISON AVENUE** Madison Avenue was one of the gated tram stops on the reserved track north of Bispham. As part of the new light rail network, the number of stops has been streamlined, to the annoyance of some North Shore residents and hoteliers, and Madison Avenue was one of the casualties. Joan and Margaret watch Brush railcoach 636 pass.

NORBECK The stretch of segregated track along the cliffs between Cabin and Little Bispham, which opened in 1898 as part of the Blackpool and Fleetwood Tramroad, remains one of the country's great tram rides. On 24 May, car 627 makes its way south from Norbreck.

Right: **NORBECK** In a similar view to the previous picture, twin-car motor 680, running singly, works a Starr Gate service on 24 May. The neo-Gothic pinnacles of the Norbreck Hydro (now the Norbreck Castle Hotel) can be seen in the distance.

Below: **LITTLE BISPHAM** In a photograph taken from railcoach 636 on 22 May, engineering car 753, converted from Standard 143 in 1958, is out on the main line south of Little Bispham.

THORNTON GATE Thornton Gate, Cleveleys, was an important permanent way depot for the Blackpool and Fleetwood tramway, on the site of former coal sidings. Until 1949 mineral wagons were hauled to the sidings by a 10-ton electric steeple-cab tram engine, now at Crich Tramway Village, from a link with the L&Y/LNWR main line behind Fleetwood's Copse Road tram depot. With its Premium Bonds roof sign, Brush railcoach 636 works towards Fleetwood on 22 May. The sidings seen here on the right have now been lifted.

1972 Happenings (1)

January
Miners vote by nearly 60 per cent in favour of a strike, which lasts seven weeks
Unemployment tops one million for the first time since the 1930s
Fourteen people are killed on 'Bloody Sunday' when troops open fire on demonstrators in Londonderry

February
The British Embassy in Dublin is burned down by protesters
Prime Minister Edward Heath declares a State of Emergency as a result of the miners' strike, which ends on 25 February
Six people are killed by an Official IRA bomb at Aldershot Barracks
US President Richard Nixon visits China

March
Ford unveils its new Granada model, which will be built at Dagenham and Cologne
The UK's last trolley bus system, in Bradford, closes
The Northern Ireland Parliament is suspended, leading to direct rule by Westminster

April
Edward Heath appoints William Whitelaw as the first Northern Ireland Secretary
Lord Chief Justice Widgery's report into Bloody Sunday clears British troops of blame because the demonstration had been illegal
The 'Brighton Belle' Pullman train makes its last journey from London Victoria to the Sussex resort

BROADWATER Photographed over the driver's arm from the cab of Coronation car 655, single-deck Brush railcoach 626 approaches the outskirts of Fleetwood at Broadwater on 19 May.

FLEETWOOD The sleek lines of Coronation car 655 make an eye-catching sight near the Ash Street tram stop (now known as Fisherman's Walk), as it returns to the depot at Manchester Square in Blackpool on 19 May.

FLEETWOOD Railcoach 633 leaves Fleetwood's street-running tracks at Ash Street for the reserved track south of the port, on its journey to Manchester Square and the depot on 19 May. The section through the centre of Fleetwood is the longest stretch of street-running track on the tramway.

1972 Happenings (2)

May

The Queen meets her uncle, the Duke of Windsor, formerly Edward VIII, at his Paris home. He dies of cancer ten days later

Ceylon becomes the Republic of Sri Lanka

The final section of the M6 opens between junctions 6 and 7 in Birmingham. The motorway stretches more than 200 miles

The Official IRA declares a ceasefire in Northern Ireland

June

A demonstration by Protestants in Londonderry turns into a battle

The Duke of Windsor's funeral takes place at Windsor Castle

118 people are killed when a British European Airways flight crashes near Staines, the UK's worst air disaster at the time

Chancellor Anthony Barber floats the pound

The Watergate burglary, which was to bring down President Nixon, takes place in Washington

July

The first official Gay Pride march is held in London

Nine people are killed and more than 100 injured in a series of IRA explosions in Belfast – 'Bloody Friday'. Ten days later, nine people die on 'Bloody Monday'

Another State of Emergency is declared after a strike by thousands of dockers

Opposite page: **FLEETWOOD** It might be spring, but North Albert Street in Fleetwood is rain-soaked as another Brush single-decker, 623, makes for the terminus past Arthur Street on 25 May.

Left: **FLEETWOOD** The positioning of the Fleetwood street tracks in the centre of the road sometimes made it tricky for waiting passengers to board. On 25 May, hopeful passengers flag down English Electric 613 at a request stop as it skims through the rain on its way to Starr Gate.

Below: **FLEETWOOD** The rain glistens on the tarmac of Lord Street, again on 25 May, as 636 nears the completion of its journey to Fleetwood. Visible on the far left is the Regent Cinema, opened in 1935 in a former Wesleyan chapel and closed in 1983, being demolished three years later. In Burton's, trousers are on sale for £2.95 a pair.

FLEETWOOD A week earlier than the previous picture, and in more spring-like weather, Coronation car 655 is at Ash Street on 19 May on its way to the terminus at Fleetwood Ferry.

FLEETWOOD At the end of North Albert Street, the double track divides for the 360-degree loop to and from Fleetwood Ferry. In unseasonal weather on North Albert Street on 25 May, Brush car 621 branches off on the curve on its way to journey's end in Fleetwood. The destination blind has already been set to Starr Gate for the return trip.

1972
Happenings (3)

Above: **FLEETWOOD** With the graceful arc of the North Euston Hotel in the background, Brush single-deck car 622 prepares for the 11-mile journey to Starr Gate on 25 May.

FLEETWOOD With track work taking place at Fleetwood Ferry, Brush railcoach 626 gingerly passes over the re-laid rails on 19 May. Behind it is the terminal for the ferry across the River Wyre to Knott End.

August

Ugandan leader Idi Amin announces that 50,000 Asians with British passports are to be expelled within the next few months

Jesus Christ Superstar, with music by Andrew Lloyd Webber and lyrics by Tim Rice, opens in London

The Palestinian Black September terrorist group storms the Munich Olympic village, killing two Israeli team members and taking nine hostage. All the hostages, a German police officer and five of the terrorists are eventually killed

September

The school leaving age is raised to 16 in England and Wales

Mastermind is first broadcast by the BBC

The Second Cod War begins after an Icelandic gunboat sinks two British trawlers

Hypermarkets make their debut in Britain when French retailer Carrefour opens a store in Caerphillly

Thousands of Ugandan Asians arrive in Britain after their expulsion by Amin

FLEETWOOD As the track work continues on the loop by Pharos Lighthouse, double-ended towing car 678 is about to start back for South Promenade 'wrong road' at Fleetwood Ferry on 19 May. Joan and Margaret (in pushchair) Ruffell watch from the pavement.

FLEETWOOD Surely the only place in the UK where trams run past a lighthouse… on 25 May, 637 is overshadowed by Fleetwood's 93ft-tall Pharos Lighthouse, opened in 1840. This area has since been attractively pedestriansed.

NORTH PIER Blackpool's illuminated trams are marvels of engineering ingenuity and adaptability. As dusk descends on 24 October, with the Lights yet to be switched on, the illuminated frigate 736 *HMS Blackpool*, converted from Pantograph car 170 in 1965 and still operational after an upgrade, the Shell Hovertram (735) and the *Blackpool Belle* paddle steamer (731) brighten the scene at North Pier.

Opposite page: **TOWER** Probably the best-loved of the Blackpool illuminated cars, the Western Train (cars 733/734) makes a spectacular sight on 25 October. The train has been magnificently restored by Blackpool Transport after a campaign by the local newspaper, *The Gazette*, led to a £278,000 grant from the Heritage Lottery Fund and re-entered service in 2008. The locomotive was built in 1962 on the remains of railcoach 209 while the trailer was a relatively simple modification of Pantograph car 174, which already had a 'Western' appearance.

1972 Happenings (4)

October
Broadcasting restrictions are lifted to allow the extension of daytime TV

John Betjeman is appointed Poet Laureate

Emmerdale Farm is first aired

Access credit cards are launched

November
The Government introduces a pay and price freeze to combat inflation

The England women's football team plays its first official match, against Scotland

The People Party, predecessor of the Green Party, is formed in Coventry

December
Eugene Cernan becomes the last man to walk on the moon, on board Apollo 17

Briton Sir John Hicks wins the Nobel Prize in Economics, with Kenneth Arrow

Fellow Briton Rodney Robert Porter is awarded the Nobel Prize in Physiology and Medicine, with Gerald Edelman

NORTH PIER Not so fortunate was the paddle steamer *Blackpool Belle*, built from 'Toastrack' 163 and modelled on a Mississippi riverboat, pictured in Talbot Square on 25 October. Withdrawn in 1978, it was shipped to Glenwood Trolley Park in Oregon, USA, but has since been stripped down for parts.

1972 Arrivals & Departures

Arrivals

Claudia Winkleman	TV presenter	15 January
Ewen Bremner	Actor	23 January
Mark Owen	Singer	27 January
Steve McManaman	Footballer	11 February
Malky Mackay	Football manager	19 February
Terry Murphy	Snooker player	6 March
Nick Frost	Actor	28 March
James Cracknell	Olympic rower	5 May
The Notorious B.I.G.	US rapper (d 1997)	21 May
Debra Stephenson	Actor	4 June
Curtis Robb	Olympic runner	7 June
Zinedine Zidane	Football manager	23 June
Geri Halliwell	Singer	6 August
Frankie Boyle	Comedian	16 August
Victoria Coren Mitchell	Writer and TV presenter	18 August
Cameron Diaz	US actor	30 August
Idris Elba	Actor	6 September
Natasha Kaplinsky	Newsreader	9 September
Jimmy Carr	Comedian	15 September
Liam Gallagher	Singer	21 September
Gwyneth Paltrow	US actor	27 September
Robert Webb	Comedian and actor	29 September
Eminem	US rapper	17 October
Samantha Janus	Actor	2 November
Danny Grewcock	Rugby union player	7 November
Ewan Birney	Scientist	6 December
Miranda Hart	Comedian and actor	14 December
Jude Law	Actor	29 December

Departures

Maurice Chevalier	French singer and entertainer	(b 1888)	1 January
Mahalia Jackson	US gospel singer	(b 1911)	26 January
John Grierson	Documentary maker	(b 1898)	19 February
Walter Winchell	US journalist and broadcaster	(b 1897)	20 February
Violet Trefusis	Writer and socialite	(b 1894)	29 February
J. Arthur Rank	Industrialist and film producer	(b 1898)	29 March
Kwane Nkrumah	Ex-president of Ghana	(b 1909)	27 April
J. Edgar Hoover	Ex-FBI director	(b 1895)	2 May
Cecil Day-Lewis	Poet Laureate	(b 1904)	22 May
Dame Margaret Rutherford	Actor	(b 1892)	22 May
The Duke of Windsor	Formerly Edward VIII	(b 1894)	28 May
Sir Francis Chichester	Round-the-world yachtsman	(b 1901)	26 August
Prince William of Gloucester	Died in an air crash	(b 1941)	28 August
Lord Geoffrey Fisher	Ex-Archbishop of Canterbury	(b 1887)	15 September
Louis Leakey	Palaeontologist	(b 1903)	1 October
Igor Sikorsky	Russian aircraft designer	(b 1889)	26 October
Ezra Pound	US poet	(b 1885)	1 November
Compton Mackenzie	Novelist	(b 1883)	30 November
L. P. Hartley	Novelist	(b 1895)	13 December
Harry S. Truman	Ex-US President	(b 1884)	26 December

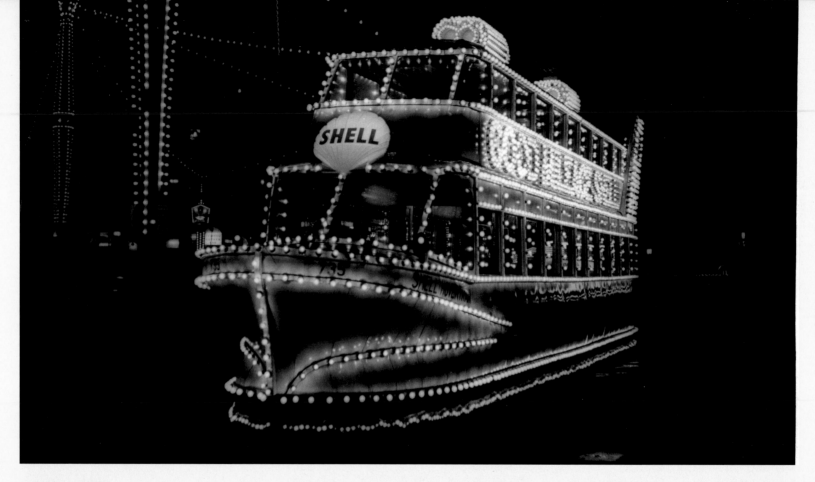

NORTH PIER Hovercraft were seen as the future in the 1960s and 1970s. On 25 October 1972, Shell Hovertram 735 makes a sparkling sight at Talbot Square. The vehicle was due to return to Blackpool in 2016 nearly ten years after leaving the resort following the signing of an initial 20-year lease with its owner, the North Eastern Electrical Traction Trust. Rebuilt in 1963 on the frames of 1935 railcoach 222, it has a capacity of 99 seats, the highest in the pre-light rail fleet. The tram, which was withdrawn in 2001, is returning for restoration by the Blackpool Heritage Trust, and it means all the surviving 1960s illuminated cars will be reunited in the resort.

Completing the illuminated fleet line-up, Trawler car 737, based on 1937 Brush car 633, was due to return to service for the 2016 Lights after overhaul at Rigby Road, following a major donation by Lofthouse of Fleetwood, manufacturer of the famous Fisherman's Friend lozenges, which the tram has advertised since its construction in 2001. The most significant part of its refurbishment, which was also supported by Fylde Tramway Society, is the replacement of the external illuminations with high-tech electronics in a joint scheme by Blackpool Transport Services and the Council's Illuminations Department.

NORTH PIER The illuminated Rocket (732) and *Blackpool Belle* near North Pier on 25 October. After being withdrawn in 1999 and later displayed as a static exhibit as the centrepiece of an Illuminations display on the roundabout at Gynn Square, the Rocket has now been moved for restoration at Rigby Road. Enthusiasts says its removal from the windswept roundabout was probably just in time as its condition was beginning to deteriorate worryingly.

NORTH PIER The Rocket, converted in 1961 from a 1928 Pantograph car and initially named Tramnik One after the Soviet Sputnik, stands ready for take-off at Talbot Square, again on 25 October. For the restorers, its unique sloping body, with passengers sitting at an angle of 20 degrees, will present challenges from an access and health and safety perspective.

NORTH PIER The row of signs advertising special tours by five illuminated trams is admired by photographer Ray Ruffell's daughter, Margaret, at Talbot Square on 27 October.

Rigby Road revealed

Below: **RIGBY ROAD** 1972 was a significant year for the Blackpool tramway with the launch of the pioneering, pay-as-you-enter OMO cars, converted from English Electric railcoaches. A gleaming car No 1, originally 616, stands inside Rigby Road depot on 25 May.

Right: **RIGBY ROAD** It might not be going to Rossall as it says on the destination blind, but the front end of new one-man operated (OMO) car No 2 makes a modernistic sight at Rigby Road on 25 May.

RIGBY ROAD New OMO cars at Rigby Road depot stand alongside their railcoach forebears, including Brush car 627, on 25 May.

Left: **RIGBY ROAD** A bunch of Balloons – if that's the correct collective noun – are gathered at the depot on 25 May, including 713 (left), 718, 703 and 700. The advertisements for Blackpool-based Empire Pools were ubiquitous on the stately Streamliners, introduced by Blackpool Corporation Tramways' legendary General Manager Walter Luff as part of his Art Deco-themed five-year modernisation plan in the mid-1930s. With their centre entrances and plush upholstery, the elegantly styled double-deckers could seat 94 passengers.

RIGBY ROAD On 14 May, the Rail Grinder and Snowplough No 2 (752), built on a truck from a Marton Box Car, and Engineering Car No 3 (753) await the call at Rigby Road. Converted from 1924-built Standard 143, with an additional diesel generator, and the centre top deck removed to accommodate an extendable inspection platform, No 3 was used for overhead line repair work. In 1961 it had its top deck ends removed and it continued in this guise until 1990 when a fire led to it being withdrawn. After work by the Lancastrian Transport Trust in the early 2000s, it returned to Blackpool Transport's Rigby Road depot in 2013 for completion of the restoration. Today it has regained its former eminence as an open-balcony Standard.

RIGBY ROAD A classic view over the inspection pits inside Rigby Road depot on 25 May. From the left are railcoaches 624, 615 and 612, towing car 679 and Balloon 713, plus one other unidentified double-decker.

Left: **RIGBY ROAD**
Stripped down to its bare bones, former English Electric single-deck car 220 is being rebuilt for one-man operation at the works in Rigby Road on 25 May.

TOWER A visit to Blackpool would not be complete without a view of the famous Tower, seen here from an interesting angle from the nearby tram stop on 14 May.

1972 Blackpool Happenings

One-man operated (OMO) trams introduced

Blackpool Zoo opens on the former Stanley Park Aerodrome

Dr Ahmad Alami murders three sleeping children at Blackpool Victoria Hospital

Superintendent Gerry Richardson, shot dead the previous year while chasing armed robbers in Blackpool, is posthumously awarded the George Cross. Inspector Carl Walker, who was wounded, also receives the medal

Tessie O'Shea and rising stars Rod Hull and Bernie Clifton appear in *The Good Old Days* at the Winter Gardens Pavilion for the summer season

At the Opera House, in the same Winter Gardens building, Cilla Black stars in the *International Spectacular '72*

Campaigners succeed in having the Grand Theatre Grade 2 listed, blocking demolition plans

Danny La Rue switches on the Illuminations in Talbot Square in September

Anthony Wedgwood Benn becomes plain Tony Benn and chairs the Labour Party conference at the Winter Gardens in October

Blackpool FC finish sixth in Division Two after being relegated the previous season, and are defeated 3-1 by Roma in their defence of the Anglo-Italian Cup

The passage of the 1972 Local Government Act signals the abolition of Blackpool's County Borough status two years later, though it was to become a unitary authority in 1998

Index of Blackpool tram types

Further reading on Blackpool from *The NOSTALGIA Collection*

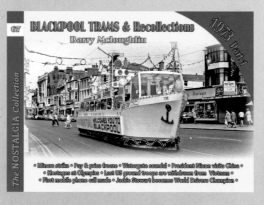
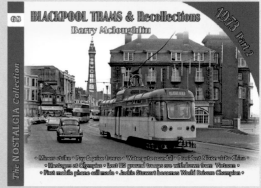
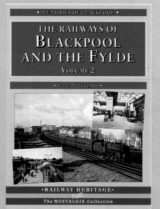
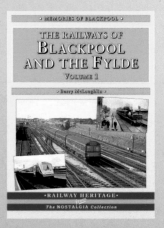

Available while stocks last – through all good booksellers